JESUS BIRTH

Truth vs assumed concepts

Chelsea Kong

© 2023 Chelsea Kong

All rights reserved. All images used in this book are licensed copies from their respectful owners including myself and Freepik, Pixabay, Pexels, Canva, and Unsplash. This book or any portion thereof may not be reproduced r used in any manner whatsoever without the express written permission of the publisher except for the use of brief quotations in a book review.

Printed in 2023, Made in Toronto, Canada
ISN: 978-1-990399-22-0
Library and Archives Canada

GOD LOVES EVERYONE BUT HE KNOWS WE ARE NOT PERFECT.
WHAT DID GOD DO?

HE LOOKED FOR A WAY TO SAVE EVERYONE.
GOD TOLD THE JEWS TO SACRIFICE ANIMALS TO HIM.

GOD, JESUS CHRIST AND HOLY SPIRIT FOUND A WAY.
JESUS AGREED TO COME TO EARTH AND BE BORN AS A MAN.

JESUS WAS BORN FROM MARY WITHOUT MAN'S BLOOD.
THE ANGEL NAMED GABRIEL TOLD HER.

GOD FOUND A MAN AND A WOMAN WHO ARE PURE.
MARY AND JOSEPH WHO BECAME JESUS PARENTS.
EVERYONE HAD TO REGISTER WHERE THEY CAME FROM.

THE WISE MAN CAME TO SEE JESUS AND BRING HIM GIFTS.
THEY FOLLOWED THE STAR TO BETHLEHEM AND MET KIND HEROD.

THE WISEMEN DID WHAT GOD SAID.
GOD TOLD JOSEPH GO TO EGYPT.
GOD TOLD HIM WHEN KING HEROD DIED.

JOSEPH STAYED LONGER IN EGYPT BECAUSE OF KING ARCHAELAUS.
THEN HE WENT BACK TO ISRAEL TO NAZARETH.
JESUS WAS CALLED A NAZARENE THERE.

MARY WAS FROM JUDAH'S FAMILY AND FROM BOAZ AND DAVID'S LINE.
JOSEPH IS ALSO FROM DAVID'S FAMILY LINE.
MARY HAS A LINK TO THE TRIBE OF LEVI THROUGH HER MOTHER.

ELIZABETH HAD JOHN FOR 6 MONTHS.
IT TOOK TIME FOR MARY TO TRAVEL TO ELIZABETH'S HOME.
ZACHARIAH WAS SERVING IN THE TEMPLE THEN.

JESUS WAS NOT BORN ON CHRISTMAS DAY.
MARY MAY HAVE MET GABRIEL IN DECEMBER.
JOSEPH KNEW MARY HAD A BABY WHEN HE SAW HER.

JOSEPH HAD TO TAKE MARY AND JESUS TO BETHLEHEM. EVERYONE HAD TO RETURN TO THEIR HOME (CENSUS OF QUIRINUS). WE MUST FOLLOW WHAT GOD TELLS US AND OBEY AUTHORITY.

JESUS MAY HAVE BEEN BORN IN A CAVE.
JESUS MAY HAVE BEEN BORN ON THE BOTTOM FLOOR OF A BUILDING.
HE WAS BORN IN THE EVENING.

THE MANGER WAS USED FOR FEEDING ANIMALS.
MARY HAD TO KEEP JESUS CLEAN AND WARM.
JESUS WAS WRAPPED IN A CLOTH FOR BABY LAMBS.

Jesus was born in Bethlehem Ephratah or Ephrathah. The city is near Rachel's tomb. (Luke 2:4, Matthew 2:1, Micah 5:2, Genesis 35:16, 48:7, Ruth 1:2, 1 Samuel 17:12).

LUKE 1:24-31 GIVES US A CLUE OF JESUS' BIRTH.
IT COULD BE MID TO LATE SEPTEMBER.
SHEPHERDS WERE AROUND WHERE JESUS WAS BORN IN THE EVENING.

JESUS MIGHT HAVE BEEN IN APRIL OR SEPTEMBER.
JESUS IS THE PASSOVER LAMB AND DIED FOR OUR SINS.
JESUS IS THE GREAT HIGH PRIEST.

JESUS IS OUR KING AND LORD OF ALL.
ANGELS CAME WHERE JESUS WAS BORN.
BETHLEHEM IS THE BIGGEST AND BRIGHTEST STAR.

JESUS BIRTH WAS A MIRACLE.
THERE WAS NO BLOOD FROM JOSEPH IN HIM.
IT TOOK A FEW YEARS FOR THE MAGI TO FIND JESUS.

THERE WERE MORE THAN 3 MAGI WHO SAW YOUNG JESUS.
THERE WERE MANY SOLDIERS THAT CAME WITH THE MAGI.
THEY THREE GIFTS ARE WORTH MILLIONS OF DOLLARS TODAY.

THE GIFTS THE MAGI GAVE MADE JESUS RICH ON EARTH.
JOSEPH AND MARY USED IT ONLY FOR JESUS.
GOD HAD TO PROTECT JESUS.

JESUS GREW UP IN GALILEE.
IT HAS A LOT OF RAIN AND WATER.
IT BECAME A GREAT PLACE FOR MERCHANTS.

MARY AND JOSEPH HAD OTHER CHILDREN.
JAMES AND JUDE ARE JESUS' HALF BROTHERS.
THEY BOTH WROTE ABOUT JESUS.

THE HOUSES HAD FOUR ROOMS.
THE HOUSE WAS TWO LEVELS HIGH.
THERE ARE STAIRS THAT GO TO THE FLAT ROOF.

THE MAGI STUDIED THE STAR OF BETHLEHEM.
THEY ARE THE WISEST MEN FROM THE FAR EAST FROM BABYLON.
THEY KNEW HOW TO READ THE STARS, PLANETS, AND SIGNS IN THE SKY.

THE STAR MIGHT BE TWO MORE STAR OR OBJECTS IN THE SKY.
STARS, PLANETS, AND OBJECTS IN THE SKY CAN WORK TOGETHER.
SCIENCE TELLS US ABOUT WHEN THEY WERE TOGETHER.

KING HEROD HAD ALL THE CHILDREN 2 YEARS OLD AND YOUNGER KILLED.
KING HEROD ANTIPAS' REIGN AND DEATH AND HIS SON ARCHALAUS' REIGN.
HISTORY ALSO HAS RECORDS OF EVENTS THAT AREN'T IN THIS BOOK.

JESUS COULD BE BORN ON THE FEAST OF TABERNACLES.
IT IS THE GREATEST FEAST FOR JEWS AND WHEN GOD DWELLS WITH US.
CHRISTIANS ALSO CELEBRATE IT TOO.

GOD'S PEOPLE WAVE THE LULAV AND ETROG TO HONOUR GOD.
THEY CALL FOR ALL THE BLESSINGS TO COME.
THEY CELEBRATE FOR 8 DAYS AND THE LAST DAY IS THE GREATEST.

GOD'S PEOPLE WILL COMMANDED TO LIVE IN TENTS.
THEY LIVE IN THEM FOR 8 DAYS.
THEY AREN'T TO DO ANY WORK AND THEY ARE TO BE UNITED.

SALVATION PRAYER

God, I know I sinned against you. Forgive me for the wrong that I have done. I believe that Jesus Christ died on the cross for me. That He rose from the grave so that after three days. I can have His long-lasting life. Come into my heart to be my Lord and Savior. I choose to turn away from my sins and I choose to follow you. Lead me to walk with you. Keep me safe and teach me your ways. Stop every bad thing in my life that has an open door to hurt me. Close those doors. Holy Spirit fill me now in Jesus' name. Amen.

BAPTISM IN THE HOLY SPIRIT

Jesus, you are the one that fills me with Your Spirit. Come Holy Spirit and come into my life and fill me to overflow with Your presence. Come with your fire too. Thank you for the gift of tongues in Jesus' name. Amen.

Open your mouth and let the words come out that God gives you. It will be words that you don't know what they mean. You can ask God what it means. You need to let Him talk through you every day to grow this gift.

He will bring you closer to God and you will know Jesus more. You will have power from God to do great things and know things.

PRAYER

Thank you, Father, thank you for Jesus' birth. Thank you for the Bible which tells about Jesus' birth. Thank you for the truth. I pray others would know when Jesus may have been born. Let me them know and find out more about Jesus' birth. Show me more about Jesus' birth in Jesus' name. Thank you Jesus that your kingdom reigns forever. Thank you that we in Christ will reign with you forever in Jesus name. Amen.

Message from the Author

The Lord has hidden secrets in the Bible that we need to ask Him what they are. Jesus' birth is in many prophecies in the Bible. God uses dreams, visions, and prophecies (words about the future) all the time, even in our life. Rabbi Jonathan Cahn has looked into the Bible to find out the secrets. We need to ask the Holy Spirit to show us and help us know what God means. Many things today are words has told through the prophets. He speaks about the future before they happen, but we may not know it. Symbols are used to tell secrets of things to come. God is always working, even when we can't see it. Everything God does follows His plan. He is always in control and knows the perfect time for everything. Names are important and lead to what God plans to do. He uses patterns too. You will find that history does repeat.

OTHER PRODUCTS

- Knowing God
- How to Hear God's Voice
- New Life in Jesus
- Loving Israel
- God's Gifts/Spiritual Talents
- Meeting God
- Word Power
- Fruit of the Spirit
- The Tabernacle
- Bride for Jesus
- A Life of Prayer
- Live Free
- Who am I in Jesus
- Walk in Love
- God's Favor
- Man of God
- Woman of God
- How to Use Money
- God's Wisdom
- Fasting
- See Jerusalem and Bethany
- First Fruit Offering
- Feast of Trumpets
- Day of Atonement
- Feast of Tabernacles
- Counting the Omer
- Festival of Lights
- Glory, Presence, and Holy Spirit
- Live in God's Presence
- Pentecost
- See Galilee, Nazareth, and Tiberias
- Hear God Speak
- Knowing Jesus
- Knowing Holy Spirit
- A Healthy Life and Healthy Life Work Book
- Smokey the Cat
- Passover Unleavened Bread
- Resurrection Life
- The Blessing
- Revival
- Chelsea Learns Hebrew
- Thanksgiving
- Give Thanks

OTHER PRODUCTS

Coming soon

Loving Jesus: Bride and Groom
Proverbs 31 Woman
Colours in the Bible
Your Daily Meal: Chelsea's Food Album
ABC's of Faith

Puzzle Books

Biblical Puzzle Book Vol 1-5
Bible Puzzles for Young Children Book 1-3
Biblical Puzzle for Children Books 1-5

Devotionals

31 Day Devotional

Inspirational/Other

Chelsea's Psalms and Poems

Teaching Series

How to Hear God's Voice Teaching Guide & Audio Book
Relationship with God, Jesus, Holy Spirit Guide
Knowing God, Jesus, Holy Spirit Guide & Audio Book
Flowing in the Prophetic

Teaching (Non-Sale on my website)

Purim

Passover

Resurrection

More books to come!

BOOK REVIEWS

More books on Amazon, Kobo, and Barnes and Noble, Smashwords, and IngramSpark.
https://chelseak532002550.wordpress.com/

More books on Amazon, Kobo, and Barnes and Noble, and Smashwords.
https://www.amazon.com/author/chelseakong

Please leave a review and share with friends to help the author continue to write more books to reach more readers. Thank you so much for your support.

Review! ★★★★★

About
CHELSEA KONG

She is a writer, creative arts and digital media artist, skilled administration professional, and podcaster. Chelsea also served in a variety of roles, from audiovisual, photography, to assisting on the worship team, and ministry team. She also has a passion for families being united.

Chelsea has been a guest on Unity Live Radio, The Lady Tracey Show, and How to Live for Christ and is highly recommended by a Proud Christian blog. She is also a guest blogger. A few of her books have been featured in YourAuthorHub, etc. She graduated from Hotel and Restaurant Management, Digital Media Arts, Office Administration, Payroll Professional, and experience working with children. Chelsea lives in Toronto, Canada. She mainly writes children's books, stories, bridal writing, poems, lyrics for songs, words of encouragement, blessings, prayers, and jokes. The author of How to Hear the Voice of God, the Bridal Collection, Knowing God, etc. She also has her own Bible Puzzle books and other inspired products. Her podcast channel is called Chelsea K on Anchor, Spotify, and iTunes.

Please check my website to find out more:
https://chelseak532002550.wordpress.com/

www.ingramcontent.com/pod-product-compliance
Lightning Source LLC
Chambersburg PA
CBHW041413010526
44107CB00016B/1153